The Way Home

Poems for the Ones Who Forgot Their Light

Ashana Kaiulani

India | USA | UK

Copyright © Ashana Kaiulani
All Rights Reserved.

This book has been self-published with all reasonable efforts taken to make the material error-free by the author. No part of this book shall be used, reproduced in any manner whatsoever without written permission from the author, except in the case of brief quotations embodied in critical articles and reviews.

The Author of this book is solely responsible and liable for its content including but not limited to the views, representations, descriptions, statements, information, opinions, and references ["Content"]. The Content of this book shall not constitute or be construed or deemed to reflect the opinion or expression of the Publisher or Editor. Neither the Publisher nor Editor endorse or approve the Content of this book or guarantee the reliability, accuracy, or completeness of the Content published herein and do not make any representations or warranties of any kind, express or implied, including but not limited to the implied warranties of merchantability, fitness for a particular purpose.

The Publisher and Editor shall not be liable whatsoever...

Made with ❤ on the BookLeaf Publishing Platform
www.bookleafpub.in
www.bookleafpub.com

Dedication

For my mother,
whose beauty and magic I always saw,
even when she couldn't see them herself.

For the girl she once was,
and the woman she never got to fully become.

May this send a wave of hope, relief,
and soft release into the world,
enough for her, and for mothers everywhere,
and for all of their children
who came here to be their own kind of special.

Preface

I didn't plan to write a book of poems.
I wrote to survive the moments that didn't have words.
Each poem started as a small prayer, or a quiet conversation with the parts of me I was learning to love again.

Over time, I began to see that these weren't just my words. They belonged to anyone who has ever lost themselves trying to be everything for everyone else. Anyone who has ever looked in the mirror and seen a stranger staring back.

This book is for the ones who have carried too much, felt too deeply, and kept showing up anyway. It's for the women who forgot their light, and for the ones who are just beginning to remember it.

You don't have to read these in order. You don't even have to understand them. Let them find you when they're meant to.

I hope these pages bring you a sense of relief, a breath of peace, or a small reminder that you were never truly lost. You were simply finding your way home.

Acknowledgements

Thank you to everyone who taught me about love by staying, and everyone who taught me by leaving.

To my children, for being my reason to soften.

To the women who trusted me with their stories, and reminded me of my own strength.

And to the light itself, for never giving up on being found.

Thank you to the silence that held me.

And thank you to the words that brought me back.

1. The Tragedy of Healing

It's not fair, you know.
That we have to stitch ourselves back together
because someone else refused to see the magic in us.

That we spend years learning
how to breathe around old ghosts,
how to love without holding our breath.

Healing sounds noble until you're in it.
Until you realize it's just grief in a prettier outfit.
Until you find yourself whispering
that you miss who you were
before you knew what this all meant.

But then, somewhere between the tears
and the trembling hands,
you feel something shift.

The smallest inhale of relief,
the gentlest warmth of being seen
by the part of you that's still here,
still choosing to stay.

2. The Hugeness of Feeling

Some of us were born
with skin that doesn't filter.

Every sound, every look, every silence
slips straight through:
a thousand small impacts
the world doesn't notice.

We feel everything.
The unspoken, the withheld,
the thing they never said but meant anyway.

We can taste tension before it's named,
hear grief hiding in someone's laugh,
sense love in the way a door closes softly.

It's a gift and a burden,
to be this porous.
To walk through life
with no armor thick enough
to keep the world from getting in.

People tell us to toughen up.
To stop taking things so personally.

To let it go.

But I've learned that feeling deeply
isn't a flaw,
it's a form of truth-telling.

Because even in the heaviness,
even when it hurts to care this much,
I would rather ache honestly
than turn myself to stone
and call that peace.

This tenderness is not weakness.
It's the pulse that proves
I'm still alive.

3. The Quiet Ones

They told us to be grateful,
to let it go, to move on..
as if moving on was a direction
you could walk toward
without leaving pieces of yourself behind.

So we learned to hold our pain like water:
carefully, quietly,
cupped in shaking hands,
trying not to spill too much
where anyone could see.

We learned how to laugh
without letting our voices crack,
how to say "I'm fine"
in a way that almost sounded true.

Inside, we built whole languages
out of glances and half breaths,
prayers no one ever taught us to speak.

And then, one day,
we saw it in someone else:
that same flicker of survival

hiding behind a calm face.

The quiet ones always find each other.
We recognize the tremble beneath the strength,
the softness that never stopped feeling,
the eyes that say,
"I see you. You're not too much.
You're just finally telling the truth."

4. The Moment You Stop Pretending

There's a silence that follows the truth.
It isn't peaceful,
it's heavy and alive,
like the air right before a storm.

You don't get applause
when you finally stop performing your pain.
No one cheers when you say,
"I'm not fine."

But that's where it starts.
That's where the old skin peels away
and the real voice crawls out,
shaky but honest.

Reminder:
You don't owe anyone beauty
while you're learning how to exist for the first time.

5. The Inconvenience of Grieving

Healing ruins your plans.
It doesn't care about your schedule
or the groceries sitting in the car.
It shows up in the middle of your to-do list
and doesn't even ask if you're ready to feel again.

You try to reason with it.
You say, *not right now, I'm busy.*
But grief is relentless.
It interrupts the conversation,
spills out in the pause between sentences,
knocks the air out of you at the sink
while the water still runs.

It lives in the half-folded laundry,
in the text you don't answer,
in the songs you skip
because they hit too close.

You start to forget
what you were saying mid-sentence.
You start to wonder
if maybe you're falling apart again.

But you're not.
You're softening.

This is the work,
the unseen labor of becoming human
in a world that keeps telling you to be steel.

Grief is inconvenient, yes.
It will make you late.
It will make you quiet.
But it will make you human.

Maybe that's our rebirth:
learning to live with a human heart
that knows both the breaking and the beauty.

6. The Way We Find Each Other

Sometimes we find home
in the unlikeliest places:
in the cracked voices
of women telling their stories
through tears that refuse to dry,
in late-night confessions
over lukewarm coffee,
in quiet nods across the room
when someone finally says the thing
we were too afraid to name.

We find it in the soft sigh
of being understood
without needing to explain.

We start to notice the same tremor
in each other's laughter,
the same pause before saying *I'm fine,*
the same exhaustion from holding it all in.

There is something holy
about the moment we realize
we are not the only ones.

That our pain has sisters.
That our strength has witnesses.

This is how we find each other:
not by pretending we are whole,
but by bringing our shaking hands
and our almost-healed hearts
to the same table,
and saying, I see you.

We don't have to be fixed
to be found.

7. The Myth of Moving On

They sold us healing as a ladder.
Climb high enough, and you'll never fall again.

But no one mentioned how slippery the rungs are,
or how easy it is to lose your footing
when a memory brushes up against your ribs.

No one tells you how often you'll circle back,
how many times you'll mistake peace for numbness,
or anger for power,
or emptiness for freedom.

Healing isn't forward motion.
It's orbit.
You return to the same places,
only each time, you meet them
with a little more gentleness.

It's learning that "moving on"
was never the goal.

You move with the ache,
with the memory,
with the version of you

who still needs time to understand.

You learn when to wade in,
when to rest,
when to let the current
carry what you can't hold.

And one day,
you realize you're not fighting the tide anymore.
You're part of it.

8. The Softening

It's strange, when it happens for the first time.
Not in a moment of clarity,
but in the quiet after a storm
that finally ran out of thunder.

You catch yourself standing there,
hands empty,
and realize the air doesn't hurt anymore.
Not the way it used to.

You don't trust it yet.
You keep waiting for the sky to split open again.
You keep one hand on the door,
just in case.

But still, you notice the light.
How it stretches across the floor
like it's been trying to find you all along.

This is the softening:
the part where you stop trying to be unshakable,
and let the world touch you without flinching.

It's not peace, not yet.

But it's close enough
to make you stay a little longer.

9. The Sacred Kind of Mad

No one talks about the rage that comes with healing.
The way it burns clean through everything polite.

Anger that builds quietly,
like pressure behind your ribs,
until even your breath tastes like smoke.

For so long I made it pretty.
I turned my pain into lessons,
into gratitude lists and silver linings,
as if that would make it easier to swallow.

But anger comes anyway.
It rises from the gut,
burning through the soft explanations
you used to survive.

This isn't hate.
It's the truth, finally unfiltered.
It's the heat that cleanses what forgiveness couldn't reach.
It's the body saying, no more.

You learn that anger has texture,

grit and pulse and memory.
It's your voice crawling back
from the places it was buried.

This is the sacred kind of mad.
The one that scorches the illusion of peace,
that clears the ground for something real to grow.

Anger is love
that finally remembered its worth.

10. The Math That Never Adds Up

After the anger,
the doubt always comes.

Maybe I imagined it.
Maybe I overreacted.
Maybe I asked for too much.

I start counting:
the times I stayed,
the things I forgave,
the parts of myself I cut away
to keep the peace.

I do the math again and again,
trying to find the number
that makes it make sense.

But it never adds up.
It never explains
why I kept shrinking to fit a story
that was never mine to hold.

Healing asks for honesty,

and honesty asks for grief,
for the years I called it love
when it was really survival,
for the ways I mistook silence
for safety.

Sometimes the truth feels cruel.
Sometimes it feels like loss.

But it's just the numbers
finally telling the truth.

And even that
is a kind of mercy.

11. My Body Knew First

Before I ever said a word,
my body was already speaking.

It flinched at footsteps,
tightened at certain tones,
forgot how to breathe in rooms
where I was supposed to feel safe.

It begged me to listen
in the only language it had:
headaches,
tension,
a heart that never rested.

I called it anxiety.
I called it tired.
I called it being too sensitive.

But the body doesn't lie.
It remembers what the mind edits out.

Every time I swallowed my truth,
it stored it in my stomach.
Every time I said "it's fine,"

it carved another knot behind my ribs.

I thought healing meant calming it down,
but now I see it was trying to protect me all along.

It knew before I did
what I could not stay for,
what I had to walk away from.

Now when it trembles,
I don't silence it.
I ask, *what are you trying to tell me?*

Because sometimes the body knows
long before the words ever catch up.

12. The Quiet Between Us

No one tells you that healing is lonely.
That the moment you start telling the truth,
the room changes.

People shift in their seats.
Their eyes wander.
They miss the old version of you:
the one who smiled through it,
the one who made everything easier to bear.

Now there's space where noise used to be.
Conversations fade.
Texts go unanswered.
Laughter feels heavier when it finally comes.

At first you think it's your fault.
You try to fill the silence,
to explain yourself into being understood.
But the quiet stays.
It's patient.
It's honest.

You start to hear things in it:
your own voice,

your own pulse,
the small relief of not pretending anymore.

This is what distance sounds like
when it's really protection.
The quiet isn't punishment.
It's the sound of space
making room for what's real.

And one day,
the loneliness softens, too.
You realize peace and isolation
can feel the same
until you learn to tell the difference.

13. The Absence of Ache

There comes a point
when even the hurting stops.
No tears.
No trembling.
Just quiet.

You think it's peace at first,
but it's not.
It's pause.
It's the body setting everything down
so it can keep you here.

The world feels distant,
like you're watching it through soft glass.
Everyone keeps moving,
and you're still,
unsure whether to call it rest or loss.

You try to cry and can't.
Try to pray and feel nothing.
Even music drifts by like wind.

This is what happens
when you've carried too much for too long.

The ache gets tired too.

And yet, inside the stillness,
something small keeps time.
A pulse.
A breath.
A low hum that says,
stay.

This isn't the end.
It's the part where life
catches up to you.
Where quiet becomes care.
Where even without feeling,
you are still being held.

14. The God of Almost

There was a time I believed easily.
Signs.
Purpose.
Timing.
All of it.

Then life started breaking faster than I could rebuild it.
Prayers went unanswered,
or maybe I just stopped knowing
how to speak the language of hope.

I tried to believe anyway,
but faith felt like a stranger in my mouth.
Every promise I repeated
sounded like something borrowed from someone else.

So I stopped forcing it.
I stopped trying to dress my pain in certainty
and started sitting with the silence instead.

That's where I found it:
the smallest something,
the God of almost.

Not the one who fixes,
or promises,
or saves,
but the one who sits quietly beside you
when you no longer know what to ask for.

The one that hums in your chest
when you whisper *I can't do this,*
and somehow,
you still do.

The one that isn't up there anymore,
but right here:
in the breathing,
the breaking,
the not giving up.

The breaking was never meant to destroy you.

It was how the light found the cracks.

16. Crying For the First Time

I didn't know the body could hold this much water.
It came in waves:
sudden, wordless,
like something ancient had been waiting
for me to stop being brave.

I cried for the little girl
who kept her siblings safe
and her grades high,
who smiled so no one would ask
if she was okay.

I cried until my eyes burned,
until I thought there was nothing left,
and then I cried for that too..
for how long it had taken me
to finally fall apart.

Grief doesn't ask for permission.
It just shows up one day
and reminds you what truth feels like
when it leaves the body.

When it was over,
I wasn't fixed.
Just emptied.
Just softer.
Just finally,
open.

17. Learning to Breathe Underwater

At first I thought I was drowning.
The world tilted,
and every breath burned.
Everything I thought would save me
was gone.

But somewhere between the gasping
and the giving up,
something shifted.
The panic slowed.
The water stopped feeling
like punishment.

I learned how to breathe differently..
not in spite of it,
but through it.

The world looked strange down here.
Quiet.
Blurry.
No rules posted on the walls.
No one watching
to tell me I was doing it wrong.

That was the hardest part:
realizing there was no one left
to get me in trouble
for saving myself.

Freedom felt heavy at first,
like a secret I hadn't earned.
But I kept breathing anyway,
awkward, unsure,
the way a newborn learns air.

Maybe this is healing?
Not climbing out,
but learning how to live
where you never thought you could.

18. The First Time I Trusted Myself

It felt wrong at first.
Like I was breaking something holy
by listening to my own voice.

For so long I waited
for someone to tell me I was allowed.
To nod.
To bless my choices.
To say, *yes, that's the right way.*

But there was no one left to ask.
Just the sound of my own breath in my ears
and the terrifying thought
that maybe I was the one in charge now.

I moved carefully,
like a child touching something fragile.
Made small decisions
and watched how my body reacted..
how it loosened or tightened,
how it whispered yes or no
without needing words.

It was humbling,
this kind of trust.
Like standing at the edge of a world
that had always been mine
but never felt safe to claim.

Some days I still look around
for someone to stop me.
To tell me I'm doing it wrong.

But no one does.
And the longer I live this way,
the more I believe
that my way
might actually be right for me.

19. Almost Believing

It started as a whisper.
A small, impossible thought.

What if I was never broken?
What if I only felt that way
because the people who were supposed to love me
didn't know how to see me?
What if I was special all along?

I tried not to believe it.
It felt too dangerous,
too proud,
too far from the shame that used to keep me safe.

But then I'd see someone else,
standing in her own light,
owning her softness,
and something in me would ache.

I believed it for her.
I believed it for everyone else
before I ever dared to believe it for myself.

That's how it happens, I think.

You catch your reflection
in another woman's bravery,
and for a second
you see your own glow
looking back.

It's quiet at first,
that kind of knowing.
It doesn't shout or prove itself.
It just sits there,
gentle and sure,
waiting for you to stop arguing.

And that's where I found my version of faith:
believing that what's sacred in them
must be sacred in me, too.

20. The Weight of My Own Life

I realized one morning:
there's no one left to tell me what to do.

No one to shame me back into smallness,
no one to clap for my compliance,
no one to call my softness a nuisance
or my truth rebellion.

For a while I didn't know what to do with that.
Freedom sounds lighter than it feels.

When you've spent your whole life
being told what's right,
what's proper,
what's good,
having no map feels like punishment.

I kept waiting for someone to step in,
to say, *that's not how you do it,*
to pull the reins.
But the silence stayed,
and in it, I heard something new:
my own direction,

quiet and sure.

It scared me,
how much it asked of me.
To trust myself,
to make peace with mistakes,
to believe that my way
could be the right way for me.

It didn't feel like power.
It felt like responsibility.
Like being handed my own heart
and told, *take care of this.*

But that's what growing up gifts us with..
realizing no one is coming,
and still choosing to live
as if you're worth showing up for.

21. A Quiet Peace

Peace didn't come with fanfare.
No lightning.
No sudden understanding.
Just a slow, steady calm
where the noise used to be.

I didn't trust it at first.
But I realized one day
that I was no longer waiting
for someone to explain it.

This is a different kind of peace
that shows up after the grief..
not joy,
not relief,
just space.

I sit in it carefully,
the way you touch something fragile
you don't want to scare away.

It feels strange to breathe
without bracing for impact.
Strange to speak

without rehearsing the apology.

This is a quiet peace:
the kind that doesn't promise forever,
only presence.

I'm learning to trust that's enough.

Not every calm is the calm before a storm.
Sometimes, it's just calm.

22. For the Girl I Used to Be

For so long,
I carried her like a secret I was ashamed of:
too tender,
too trusting,
too full of love for a world
that never knew what to do with her.

I used to fear her softness.
I thought she made me weak.
I thought survival meant becoming someone
she wouldn't recognize.

But healing has a way of circling back.
And lately,
I've been finding her everywhere..
in the way I laugh without hesitating,
in the songs I forgot I loved,
in the small, stubborn ache for goodness
that never went away.

Sometimes I still cry for her.
For what she saw,
for what she lost,
for how long she had to wait

for someone to come for her.

But when I picture her now,
I don't see a wound.
I see a bright light,
still burning,
still believing,
still mine to protect.

So I tell her,
I'm here now.
You don't have to earn love anymore.
You get to rest.

And together,
we learn what that means.

23. Letting Someone Close

I didn't trust softness anymore.
Every kind word felt like bait.
Every promise made my stomach tighten.

Love had been the doorway
that pain walked through too many times.

So when someone offered simple kindness,
nothing owed,
nothing demanded,
I didn't know what to do with it.

I waited for the switch.
Waited for the silence.
Waited for the mask to slip.

But it didn't.
There was no explosion,
no collapse.

Just warmth.
Steady presence.
Shared laughter that didn't cost me anything.

I didn't know connection could sound like that:
quiet,
ordinary,
safe.

I still flinch sometimes.
Still brace for the ending.
But I keep letting the moment stretch,
a little longer each time.

And when it's over,
I notice the air:
how it stays soft and open
even after the conversation is over.

Friendships like this can change everything, quietly.

24. Belonging

There's also a sense of peace
in not needing a crowd.

I used to ache for it:
the easy laughter,
the automatic plans every Saturday,
the feeling of being someone's person.

But these days,
belonging feels smaller.
Quieter.
A person
who see the same storms in me
and doesn't flinch.

We don't talk every day.
We don't need to.
There's trust that lives beneath the silence,
steady and sure.

My home isn't built from numbers anymore.
It's made of presence.
Of people who stay
without needing to be convinced.

I used to think I'd feel lonely
with quiet around me.
Now it feels just right:
enough room to breathe,
enough truth to stay.

25. Coming Home

Presence is an experience.
I'll be walking through my house
and suddenly feel the weight of being here.

The light hits the floor just right,
or the sound of my own footsteps
feels like proof.

Nothing dramatic,
but a quiet awareness
that I'm not waiting anymore.

Not scanning.
Not listening for danger.
Just here.

It doesn't rush in.
It doesn't even feel good, exactly.
It's steadier than that.
Clear.
Real.
Solid.

For a second, I can absorb the whole picture:

the room,
my body,
my breath,
my posture,
and it all makes sense.

This is what safe feels like.
No prerequisite of joy,
no requirement of relief,
just presence.

The simple truth
of being fully alive
and knowing it.

26. Ordinary Things

Lately I've been catching myself mid moment
doing something small,
like pouring my daughter a bottle
or folding a towel still warm from the dryer..
and realizing I'm here.

No one watching.
No one waiting for me to fail.
Just the soft vulnerability of living
without armor.

The air feels different now.
I notice how it flows into my lungs,
how time doesn't rush me anymore.

I used to think healing would feel holy,
like revelation or rebirth.
But it's this instead:
the steady existence of ordinary things,
the quiet awareness of nothing being wrong.

It's the way the house holds me
without needing a reason.
The way I sometimes dance along to a song

before I realizing I'm doing it.

I don't think peace announces itself.
I think it just starts showing up
in the middle of your life,
catching you unawares in bits and pieces
until one day
you realize you've stopped preparing
for it to end.

27. The Name I Kept

For a long time
I answered to versions of myself
that never quite fit.

The mature one.
The strong one.
The girl who could take it.

Each name came with a script:
how to act,
how to shrink,
how to make everyone comfortable.

I carried them like costumes,
switching shapes
to match the room.

But lately,
I've been speaking my own name
out loud,
slowly,
without apology.

It feels strange on my tongue,

familiar and foreign at the same time.
Like finding an old song
I used to love
and realizing I still know the words.

I don't need to explain it anymore.
I don't need to make it easier to swallow.

This is who I am.
This is who I've been
the whole time.

28. The Crying Days

Some days, I cry at everything.
Not because anything's wrong,
but because my body is finally learning
what it means to let go.

A song, a smell,
the sound of my child laughing
from another room..
it all unravels me a little.

There was a time
I treated tears like a threat,
something to brace against,
to lock away behind clenched teeth.

I swallowed them with my dinner,
felt them travel down my throat:
a secret no one wanted to hear.

Now they come easily.
They rise and fall
like waves that finally know
they won't be punished for existing.

It doesn't feel dramatic anymore,
just much needed.
A felt relief
I didn't know I was starving for.

Even when it aches,
there's something sacred about it:
the way sorrow softens into gratitude,
how the pain hums underneath my peace
instead of replacing it.

Some days I cry for everything I lost,
some days I cry because I survived.
Both feel like prayer.

29. What I Know Now

Peace isn't the absence of pain.
It's the space that holds it
without collapsing.

Healing doesn't erase what happened.
It teaches the body
how to stay.

I don't need to be understood
to be real.
I don't need to be forgiven
to be free.

Grief still visits,
but it doesn't barge in anymore.
It knocks,
and I answer kindly.

The child in me still cries,
and I know how to hold her.
I don't rush to make her quiet.

Joy doesn't shout either.
It harmonizes.

It hides in the corners of my day
and waits to be noticed.

None of it is perfect,
and I don't want it to be.
Perfection was never going to bring me peace.

What I know now
is that I can live inside the mess
and still call it beautiful.

30. Coming Home

Sometimes I think about the little girl I used to be,
the one who believed everything good
was still ahead of her.

She said she'd have six kids one day.
She said it with the kind of certainty
that only innocence can explain.
And I laughed at her,
years later,
when life felt too hard
to make room for that kind of dreaming.

But here I am:
five small souls who call me home,
each one proof
that she was right to believe in something bigger.

She would be proud, I think.
Not because it's perfect,
but because I kept going.
Because I found joy
in places we didn't know existed.

I wish I could tell her

how much she got right..
how much she already knew
about love,
about grit,
about the way we'd build a life
out of everything that tried to break us.

I used to think coming home
meant finding constant calm.
But it's this:
standing in the middle of my real life,
hands full,
heart full,
and knowing we made it.

31. To the One Still Healing

If you're still in it..
the sleepless nights,
the racing thoughts,
the grief that hides in ordinary days..
this is for you.

You haven't failed because it still hurts.
You haven't missed your chance at peace.
You're just human,
and healing can take longer than anyone admits.

Some days you'll be proud of how far you've come.
Other days, you'll wonder if you've changed at all.
Both are true.
Both count.

You don't have to forgive before you're ready,
or make meaning out of what broke you.
Some things just happened.
And that's enough reason to rest.

Please don't rush your becoming.
Softness will return in its own time.
So will laughter.

So will trust.

Until then, keep breathing.
Keep choosing yourself
in the smallest, quietest ways.

Peace isn't waiting on the other side of this;
it's being built in you,
slowly,
every time you decide to stay.

. The Light That Stays

I don't have neat answers.
Just proof that we can live through things
and still love what comes next.

If you saw yourself anywhere in these pages,
thank you for reading along.

I hope you find your way home,
however it looks.

If you'd like to keep exploring these themes,
you can listen to my podcast, *The Reclamation Room,*
where I share stories and conversations
about the work of coming home to yourself.

You can also find me on social media at *Way Home Wellness,*
where I write, teach, and hold space for women
doing this work.

You're always welcome to join my circle;
it's where the conversation continues.
The healing journey is the human condition,
and the best part is, you don't have to do it alone.

www.ingramcontent.com/pod-product-compliance
Lightning Source LLC
Chambersburg PA
CBHW060352050426
42449CB00011B/2948